Space Voyager

Jupiter

by Vanessa Black

Bullfrog Books

Ideas for Parents and Teachers

Bullfrog Books let children practice reading informational text at the earliest reading levels. Repetition, familiar words, and photo labels support early readers.

Before Reading

- Discuss the cover photo. What does it tell them?

- Look at the picture glossary together. Read and discuss the words.

Read the Book

- "Walk" through the book and look at the photos. Let the child ask questions. Point out the photo labels.

- Read the book to the child, or have him or her read independently.

After Reading

- Prompt the child to think more. Ask: What are your favorite facts about Jupiter?

Bullfrog Books are published by Jump!
5357 Penn Avenue South
Minneapolis, MN 55419
www.jumplibrary.com

Library of Congress Cataloging-in-Publication Data

Names: Black, Vanessa, 1973–author.
Title: Jupiter / by Vanessa Black.
Description: Minneapolis, MN : Jump!, Inc., [2018]
Series: Space voyager
"Bullfrog Books are published by Jump!."
Audience: Ages 5–8. | Audience: K to grade 3.
Includes bibliographical references and index.
Identifiers: LCCN 2017026844 (print)
LCCN 2017033280 (ebook)
ISBN 9781624966842 (e-book)
ISBN 9781620318409 (hardcover : alk. paper)
ISBN 9781620318416 (pbk.)
Subjects: LCSH: Jupiter (Planet)—Juvenile literature.
Classification: LCC QB661 (ebook)
LCC QB661 .B53 2017 (print) | DDC 523.45—dc23
LC record available at https://lccn.loc.gov/2017026844

Editor: Jenna Trnka
Book Designer: Molly Ballanger
Photo Researchers: Molly Ballanger & Jenna Trnka

Photo Credits: NASA images/Shutterstock, cover, 8, 23ml; Rawpixel.com/Shutterstock, 1; Veronica Louro/Shutterstock, 3 (boy); Polina Valentina/Shutterstock, 3 (drawing); B.A.E. Inc/Alamy, 4; JPL-Caltech/SwRI/MSSS/Gerald Eichstadt/Sean Doran/NASA, 5, 23tl; Stocktrek Images/Alamy, 6–7; JPL/NASA, 9, 15; Walter Myers/Stocktrek Images/Alamy, 10–11; JPL/DLR/NASA, 12–13; Tristan3D/Shutterstock, 14; Dominic Hatcher/Alamy, 16–17, 23mr; janez volmajer/Shutterstock, 18–19, 23tr; Artsplav/Shutterstock, 20–21; adventtr/iStock, 23bl; Fotos593/Shutterstock, 23br; muratart/Shutterstock, 24.

Printed in the United States of America at Corporate Graphics in North Mankato, Minnesota.

Table of Contents

The Big One

What is the fifth
planet from the sun?

It is big.

It is made of gas.

It is Jupiter!

Look at our solar system.

Jupiter is the
biggest planet.

How many Earths
could fit inside?

1,300!

Jupiter

Earth

Jupiter has a red spot.
What is it?

red spot

A big storm.

Jupiter has rings.

They are made
of dust and rocks.

They are hard to see.

rings

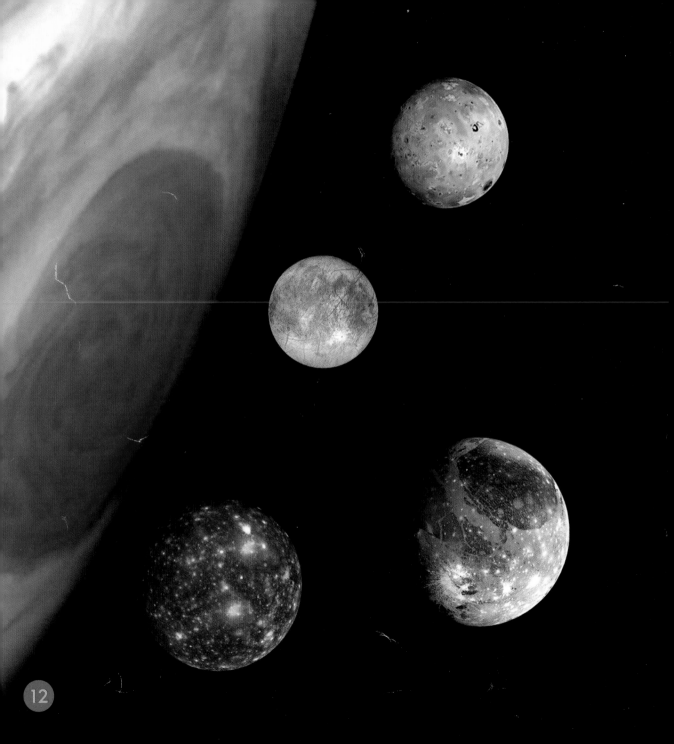

Jupiter has many moons.

How many?

More than 50!

Io is one.

It has volcanoes.

**Europa is another.
It is mostly water.**

15

How do we know?

We use telescopes.

We see far away.

We send out spacecraft.
They take photos.

Wow!
What do you like about Jupiter?

A Look at Jupiter

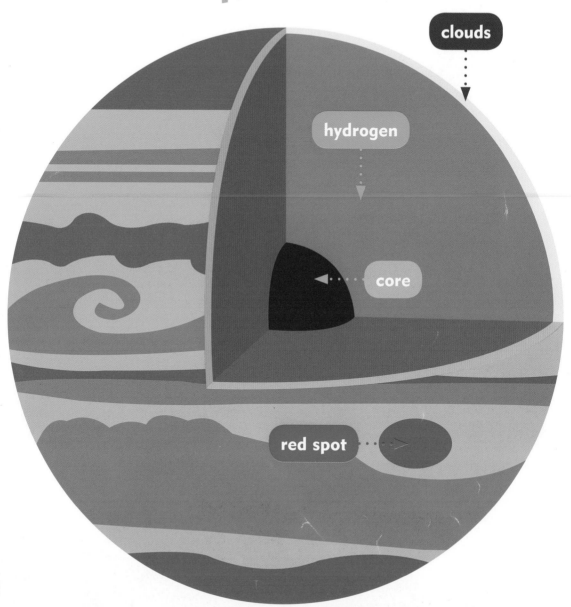

clouds

hydrogen

core

red spot

Picture Glossary

gas
A substance similar to air that expands to fill space.

spacecraft
Vehicles that travel in space.

planet
A large body that orbits the sun.

telescopes
Instruments that allow us to view distant objects.

solar system
The sun and other planets that revolve around it.

volcanoes
Vents in the crust of a planet that can spew lava and steam.

Index

To Learn More

Learning more is as easy as 1, 2, 3.

1) Go to www.factsurfer.com

2) Enter "Jupiter" into the search box.

3) Click the "Surf" button to see a list of websites.

With factsurfer.com, finding more information is just a click away.